CW01668553

101 ways to cope with grief & loss

Bill Merrington

kevin mayhew

Published in 2007 by

KEVIN MAYHEW LTD
Buxhall, Stowmarket, Suffolk, IP14 3BW
E-mail: info@kevinmayhewltd.com
www.kevinmayhew.com

ISBN 978 1 84417 789 9
Catalogue No. 1501016

Cover design by Sara-Jane Came
Edited by Linda Ottewell
Typeset by Richard Weaver

In memory of
my mother, father and grandmother,
whose deaths forced me to face my own grief,
that I might survive and indeed thrive.

Contents

Finally

Introduction

When you experience the death of someone who was close to you, there begins a process that no one can stop. Whether you like it or not, you find yourself at the beginning of a journey. It is a venture that seems out of control. There seem to be no road signs along the way and everyone else seems to be on a different path. The journey seems to have no end, with ups, downs and detours that come upon you without warning. On top of this, there seems to be no atlas or map to direct you.

Having supported, counselled and cared for many bereaved people over the years, I have to acknowledge I cannot fully understand what you are experiencing. My experience of loss is different from yours. We all come with different personalities, family backgrounds, intensity of relationships and experiences of previous losses in life. All of this will shape and alter how we react to our present situation. But this does not mean there is nothing we can do about our condition. Even when we want to do nothing about the circumstances we find ourselves in, we can at least acknowledge where we find ourselves.

So how can we help ourselves? This book gives small signposts to guide and aid you on your journey. Some will help you think through your loss experience, others will aid you practically, while some will simply give you a focus to get through the week. You can work through the book systematically or simply dip into it at will. All I ask is that you persevere, working through each chapter. Perhaps you could just read one page each day.

There will be times when this book will annoy you, when you don't want to face the issue at hand, or it produces so much pain and heartache that you feel you can't continue. But there will be other days when you might feel as if you want to read the book right through in one day. Simply acknowledge that you are on a journey, whether you like it or not, and be willing to keep on thinking through the issues raised. You may find that as the months go by, your opinion changes as you read each chapter, so be willing to look again at the pages and reassess your view. Any journey of grief will involve times of upset and pain. You are not alone in this experience but be assured that there is light at the end of the tunnel, however dim it might seem.

Each section finishes with some 'tips'. See if you can carry out some of the ideas and suggestions, as it will give you something constructive to do.

Let the journey begin . . .

Starting the journey

1 *It's OK to grieve*

We live in a society where we expect answers to all our questions. If ill, we look to the doctors for answers. But when we experience the death of a relative or friend, we find ourselves thrust into an emotional and physical turmoil.

Let's first clarify some terms: bereavement = grief + mourning.

Bereavement is what happens to us when someone close to us dies. Grief is the emotional reaction that results, whether we like it or not. Mourning is how we react socially, within a particular environment and culture.

Secondly, let us acknowledge that grief is not an illness, but a natural, normal reaction that can be found throughout the world. Don't fight it, but accept the fact that this is what happens to all humans when we experience the death of a person close to us. Whether we like it or not, we have embarked on a journey. Some have seen it rather like a train journey. You get on the train, and sooner or later you arrive at a destination and get on with your life. Here you are almost an observer of what happens to you. Others see it rather as a car journey. Here, you control the route and the speed of the journey. More recently, grief theorists are recognising that grief is perhaps more like a walk, which for some takes a lifetime. You will form your own view eventually, but for now just acknowledge that you are on a journey. Many have journeyed this way before, but your journey will be unique to you. You cannot stop it, but you can influence the speed and the route.

Make yourself a drink, sit down and tell yourself: it's OK to grieve.

2 *We all need TLC*

Some of us are extroverts, others are introverts; some prefer to be active and on the go all the time, while others prefer to find space to think and to be. But whatever your personality make-up might be, none of us is an island. We all need support, both from family, friends and those who can identify with our loss. It might be practical help like doing your ironing, making some food for the freezer or collecting the children from school. It might be simply sitting with us and listening to our story. By accepting help, it can provide space for you to focus upon what is important – accepting the death. The mind is racing, the body is in shock, and our normal routine has been thrown up in the air. Surely we deserve a little help? If there ever was a time when you should be kind to yourself, it is when you are adjusting to the death of a relative or friend.

Now if you are like me, and you need your space and you find it hard to accept help, don't despair. But even those of us with this temperament could benefit from a little help, even if it is from just one or two select people.

Imagine you are on a trampoline,
being thrown up and down.
Who would you want to be standing by the side,
ready to catch you?
Make a list of your key supporters.

3 *Acknowledge why we grieve*

Someone once said to me, 'Bill, sort me out quickly. I don't want to bother with all this grief stuff.' Unfortunately, although you have some control of your grief journey, you cannot detour or bypass normal grief reactions. Thank goodness, because there is a good reason why we react the way we do. Grief is the price we pay for loving and caring. You might like to see it as a by-product of love. Thousands of people die every day, but most of us are not affected by it. It is only when someone dies where we have formulated a close bond. That doesn't mean that the relationship was perfect, or without problems. Think of a relationship rather like having an elastic band between two people. The thickness of the band will depend upon how close or complex the relationship is. For many, the longer the relationship, the thicker the band becomes. (The band between a parent and a baby or child starts life as being very thick.) When death occurs, the band snaps and three things happen. First, we try to escape the pain caused as the band breaks. Secondly, we try to repair the band. Finally, we try to make sense of it all. These three things play a significant role in our journey of grief. So don't fight this experience that you are encountering, but recognise that it is because of the commitment, time and perhaps the love that you have placed into this relationship, which results in this painful experience.

Acknowledge to yourself how important this bond that has snapped was to you.

4 *Build a road map*

A road map is a simple picture or diagram of the events that have happened to you. You can make it on a piece of A4 paper or on larger drawing paper. Don't panic, you don't have to be able to draw or paint. Think of a map of where you live. It contains all sorts of information: places you've been and places you have yet to visit. You will also see a road that you have travelled perhaps many times. The events of your loss are like this road. So try and draw a road of your past journey. Begin with a positive memory before any thought of loss entered your world. Put different markers/road signs on the map of what happened to you: the things that were significant to you. It might include places, people, thoughts and questions. The map you produce can be simply words, or you might like to draw it and use coloured pictures. Roll the map up and keep it safe. It is your own story and experience. No one can disagree with it. It's yours. However, you might like to share the map with someone you trust. Talk it through, explaining what is important to you. You may find you want to make additions to the map as you remember different significant moments.

Find some space to yourself to do this exercise.
Take your time and keep coming back to it
to make any additions.

5 *A punctured tyre*

There was once a time when you would see lots of cars waiting for the AA or RAC on the slip-road of a motorway. Today, we may see this less often, but engines still break down and tyres still get punctures. The rules haven't changed. The tyre will not get fixed by itself. It's the same with grief. There are two misconceptions about loss. When we are bereaved, people will often say, 'Pull yourself together,' or 'You'll get over it,' or 'Don't think about it.' They can treat you as if you have a cold which just needs shaking off. But grief is 100 per cent. It infiltrates every part of your being, time and space. It has to be taken seriously. That doesn't mean there is nothing you can do about it, however. A second common reaction is to say, 'Time will heal.' But time doesn't heal anything. Someone has to fix a flat tyre and re-inflate it. Grief is the same; it requires your input to work through many issues and feelings if you are to feel re-inflated and back functioning as normal. Now I can hear you replying, 'I don't want to be back to normal.' That's OK, but no one wants to sit by the roadside forever. When you are ready, and you can decide when, it's time to pick up the phone and dial the AA or RAC. In a sense, that's what you are doing right now, reading this book. Well done, you are acknowledging that something serious has happened to you and you are doing something about it.

Picture a broken-down car by the roadside.
Can you relate to this?
Acknowledge to yourelf that you will need to
take action eventually.

6 Complete the picture

When someone dies, there is a sense of disbelief. Even when we have had time to be aware that the person was dying, we can still find the loss hard to take in. Until we come to terms with the fact that our loved one has died, we will not be able to move forward. Information helps us to begin to make sense of it all. It can be helpful, therefore, to find out where, when, how and why a person died. This might involve talking to the doctor or hospital, the coroner, or someone who was there at the point of the death. We may have been given information previously, but were not able to retain the knowledge because of the pressure of the moment. It does no harm to go back and recap, so that you can be sure you have the full picture of what has occurred.

Make a list of what questions you may still have that require answers.

7 *GPs and tranquillisers*

In the early part of your journey of grief, you may find yourself going to the doctor more often than previously. This is very normal. The emotional shock of loss leads to a variety of physical symptoms, e.g. headaches, heart palpitations, loss of appetite, digestive problems, dizziness, nightmares, lack of sleep, constriction of throat, muscular pain, impeded concentration, poor memory, damp hands and dry mouth. You have good reason to visit the doctor. However, there is good news. These symptoms are not serious and, on the whole, do not last long. They reflect the overload that the mind has to cope with as it adjusts to the loss. This raises the question: should I take tranquillisers? Doctors have a natural desire to help with your symptoms and will often offer aids to help you sleep and relax. They can help initially if you are struggling to get to sleep. However, eventually the mind has to work through all the issues relating to the grief. It is important that you don't get trapped using tranquillisers, which later can be difficult to stop taking. Keep talking to your doctor and come to an agreement on the best way of weaning you off the pills. The doctor may offer you bereavement counselling. This is very helpful, but often people are sent to counsellors too early in the grief experience. Counselling is no magic wand to take away the pain. However, after three to six months, counselling can be very supportive.

Decide to talk this through with your doctor.

8 *Find your support group*

When we have experienced one loss, it naturally makes us anxious for others in our lives. When death has entered our home, we can fear it might return. This can make us feel that we are alone with our thoughts and experiences. However, the reality is often so different. On a piece of paper, write your name at the centre. Make a series of circles around you. In each circle, write down the people closest to you. Your closest friends and family first, and then as you move outwards, all the people who relate to you. Build the list up, until you have a full list of all the people in your life. Remind yourself daily of this list, think about a particular person and why they are special to you. Reassure yourself that you are not alone.

You will find that among your friends and relatives, there are some who cope well with your grief and loss, while others will find it just too hard to handle. We are all different, just don't judge too harshly those who keep their distance.

It is not unusual for bereaved people to find new friends who understand and can empathise with you. Remember, friends are there to lean upon; make the most of them, for one day they may need you.

Make a phone call and thank your friends for just being there when you need them.

9 *Dark days*

We all feel a little better when the weather is sunny and bright and we are able to get outside. But when winter arrives, the clocks go back and the dark nights draw in. Many can feel negative and even depressed during the winter months. When we are bereaved, the winter can seem the worst time of all. When you are waking to darkness and drawing the curtains by five o'clock in the afternoon, you can feel very alone and isolated. We can't change the weather but we can at least recognise that this is a difficult time. Let friends know, as they may not realise. Perhaps get someone to ring you in the evenings rather than in the day-time. If friends are calling, ask them to come when you would value their company the most. Save special treats for the evening so that it might be a pick-me-up for you. Don't put a strain upon yourself by expecting to achieve a lot in the evening. Target important jobs for the daytime. This means that by the evening, you can at least feel you have achieved something during the day.

Plan now how you will handle and prepare for going to bed.

10 *Sleep*

When your mind is racing with so many thoughts and worries, it is understandable that sleep can be difficult for the bereaved. Often the anxiety of the day will make you feel tired but when it comes to bed, somehow the mind will just not shut off. We all have our own pattern of how to get to sleep, so it is best to stick with what we know. But if this doesn't work, then there are a few simple steps that can help. First, we must focus upon the daytime. Try not to sleep in the day. Bereaved people often find at first they are so exhausted that they get into the habit of sleeping at different times. But try to save your sleep for the night-time. Secondly, try and fit into the day some kind of gentle exercise and fresh air. If you keep heavier meals for lunch and have lighter snacks at teatime, it will help the body be ready to relax at night. If you visit the toilet often at night, try to limit your drinking in the evening. At night-time, go to bed on good terms with yourself. The annoyances and irritations of the day don't make good bedfellows. Say goodnight to your loved one. This is a way of drawing a line under all your thinking of the day. If you are inclined, read before you sleep. This focuses the mind on something other than the events of the day. If you are struggling to sleep, or wake up and can't get back to sleep, then don't just lie there. It's better to get up for a warm, non-caffeine drink and then read for about half an hour before going back to bed.

Reflect upon whether you need to make any changes to your sleep pattern.

11 Dreams

As we busy ourselves during the day, we somehow get through hour by hour. We are like a boat bobbing up and down on the sea, tossed to and fro by the waves. At times there seems to be no horizon and we are unclear where we are heading. How do we make sense of all that we are going through? For the bereaved, dreams can be the world that lies below the water level. Some people tend not to remember their dreams, while others will recall vivid dreams of the deceased. The dream can seem so real that there is a reluctance to let the dream end. In that special moment, we are able to have our loved one back with us. When the dreams cease, we can feel let down. Sometimes in couples, just one partner dreams of the deceased, which leaves the other one feeling left out. Sometimes dreams seem such a torment that it stops you wanting to go to sleep.

Dreams are not a by-product of sleep but rather an opportunity to work through issues yet to be resolved on the conscious level. It can therefore be helpful to keep a journal by your bedside and to write down any of the dreams that you recall. There are counsellors who would be able to talk through the issues that the dreams raise. But simply making a note of the dreams and reflecting upon them later may well be enough for you.

Get a note pad and put it by the bedside with a pencil or pen.

12 *Find your first-aid kit*

Most people have some kind of first-aid kit in the house. You might like to get yours out and look at what it contains: scissors, plasters, bandages, ointments, etc. We need a first-aid kit to care for us physically when we are hurt, but what do we use when we are emotionally hurt in grief? A first-aid kit is there to help us when in need. So let's think through our own emotional first-aid kit. What will it consist of? On a piece of paper, draw or write a list of what is in your first-aid kit for physical pains and then make a list of your emotional kit. It might consist of people you turn to when in need, people who are good at listening to you, others who are better at practical jobs. You might have a favourite place to go to that has special memories, or a special object that comforts you. It might include comfort food, clothes you feel good in or a telephone number you know you can ring if in need. A special piece of music, a favourite book or poem can be very comforting. Pin the first-aid kit up on a wall where you can see it and use it when necessary. Remember, it is there to be used.

If you haven't got a first-aid kit in the house,
why not go and get one?

13 Learn to say 'no'

When was the last time you said 'no'? We teach children to say 'no' to strangers or anything that is not good for them, but we are not good at doing it ourselves. How often are we asked a casual or innocuous request and find ourselves saying 'yes' when we really wanted to say 'no'? When life is good, such situations may annoy us, but in the end it is not too much trouble. However, when we are under the weather and having to cope with a turmoil of emotions and thoughts, saying 'yes' is the last thing we might want to do. There are many circumstances when it's right to say 'no', but especially if you are feeling overburdened. In the end it will affect you more than the person making the request. It is up to you to make sure you do not become run-down and overtired. It takes practice to say 'no' and some of us find it harder than others. But saying 'no' firmly and politely can be transforming. Remember, now is the time to look after yourself. Let the problems of the world look after themselves for a change, they'll cope. Be brave and have a go.

Is there something you could give up?
Pick up the phone and cancel it.

Tried and tested rules

14 *Breakfast first, please*

We all have our morning rituals when we wake. Some of us are morning people while others prefer the evening. But when we are under the weather, we need to think carefully how we look after ourselves. We know, regardless of feelings, that breakfast people enjoy better moods, higher energy levels throughout the morning and better performance at school and at work. Skipping breakfast just gets the day off to a bad start and can be the beginning of a series of negative effects. Eating first thing in the morning stabilises your blood sugar and regulates your energy levels. If you can't be bothered for yourself, then have breakfast at least for your loved ones who would want you to look after yourself. Tell them you have had a good breakfast and they'll stop worrying as much about you.

For some, the empty space at the table is upsetting. So treat yourself and take your breakfast to another cosy spot. In the winter find somewhere warm and relaxing, perhaps with the TV on or music playing. Taking your breakfast to bed is allowed! In the summer, weather permitting, why not try sitting outside and breathe in the fresh air?

Tomorrow morning treat yourself
to your favourite breakfast.

15 *Eat your greens*

It is very natural, when you are feeling low, to lose your appetite. However, this has a knock-on effect. When we fail to eat healthily, it affects our physical well-being, which in turn affects us emotionally. We can find ourselves in a vicious circle of decline, which can lead to more minor physical ailments. Sometimes we just need to eat healthily whether we feel like it or not. Begin by filling the kitchen with fruit, vegetables and a few of your favourite things. If cooking is too much of an effort, try cooking something simple and quick, like pasta. At first, you may find that most of what you prepare is thrown away. That's OK at first. Keep nibbling and nibbling until your appetite comes back. If previously you would have prepared food for the deceased, it is very natural to cook excess food, as if you are cooking for two. Why not ask a friend over, make it lunchtime and prepare some food for them. To eat and chat can be easier than eating alone. Give yourself a focus for one week to work at eating healthily and often.

Make a list of what would be good to buy this week.

16 *Fresh air is free*

When life has been turned upside down, we can find ourselves not carrying out our normal routine. This can lead to a lack of physical exercise. This, along with a poor diet, can lead to our health declining and lowers our resistance to infection. All of this can make us feel more trapped in the home where we withdraw further from society. At times we can feel rather like an artist stuck with a blank piece of paper in front of us, or a computer operator where the computer is stuck on screen-saver. We need a way of breaking out of the mould we find ourselves in. Bereaved people constantly tell me that a simple walk taking in fresh air proved to be one of the best aids to get them through difficult times. You may prefer to walk with a friend or to be on your own. Either way it allows the physical body to exercise and being in the open air can allow the mind to get a different perspective on life. Start off with a gentle, short walk and see whether you can extend it over the week. Sometimes your mind may be blank and at other times it may be racing with too much to think about. That's OK, remember the walk is to help you physically; in time it will help you mentally and emotionally as well.

Phone a friend and ask them to walk with you.

17 *Keep fit*

Keeping fit is probably the last thing you feel like at the moment. But if you asked any doctor, they would suggest some sort of gentle exercise. Why not ask the doctor for a health check and see what he or she recommends? If you have not done any sort of activity for some time, it is important to build up slowly. Any aerobic or cardiovascular exercise will strengthen the heart and improve the blood flow taking oxygen to the rest of the body. Swimming or just gentle walking can make a world of difference, not only physically but also mentally. Pilates or yoga classes might suit you better if you are not keen on swimming. Exercise can increase self-confidence and give you more energy for the tasks ahead of you. Doing the exercise with a friend can help you to persevere with it at the times when you feel least like going. It also gets you out of the rut of being trapped in the house all the time. If you are back at work, then going to a gym or swimming baths is a good way of relaxing and getting the day's events out of your system.

Check out swimming baths/pilates or yoga class times.

18 *Doing small jobs*

I have a hobby of woodcarving head busts. It's a time-consuming hobby, but the hardest part of the whole exercise is when I am faced with a big square chunk of wood. Sooner or later I have to be willing to take the chisel and remove a small chip of wood. Before I know it, a head is appearing, which encourages me to complete the project.

There are times when you can look around the house or at work and see so many jobs to do, that it all seems overwhelming. The good news is that many jobs just don't need to be done, or they can wait for another day, or someone else can do them. It reminds me of the saying, 'How do you eat an elephant?' The answer is simple, 'A bit at a time.' I appreciate that no one wants to eat an elephant, but you would if you were hungry enough; needs must. Eventually, there will be tasks that have to be completed, however difficult they might be to you. Instead of seeing these tasks as enormous weights, try breaking them down into small jobs that you can chip away at a bit at a time. Get someone close to you to help you decide what is the most urgent; you can then prioritise the rest. This releases the mind from worrying about so many things and in turn helps your own well-being.

Is there one thing you can do today
that will make you feel better?

19 *Keep a diary*

Journals can contain ideas, thoughts, moans, prayers, pencil sketches, calendar dates and drafts of furious letters. Every day you will have different thoughts, memories and questions shooting through your head. To help, it can be beneficial to write down your thoughts and feelings. Using a diary or a notebook on a daily basis gives a focus to the many thoughts that you may have. Rather than keep these feelings trapped in the mind, writing them down can be a form of release. As the months or years progress, you can look back at your experience and see how you have moved on in your thoughts, feelings and attitude.

Today, what can you write down about your thoughts, feelings and questions?

20 *Questions, questions, questions*

When loss comes into your life, it is as if a jigsaw has been thrown up into the air for no apparent reason, with the pieces falling all over the place and some going missing. It is understandable that we therefore feel very disorganised. We all shy away from pain and will do what we can to avoid the pain of loss. We don't want to believe that the jigsaw is in pieces. We do all we can to frantically put the pieces back together, not wanting any piece to be lost. But in the end it seems we just cannot find each and every piece. We are left trying to understand why it happened and where the pieces have gone and we have many unanswered questions. These questions can easily get stuck in our heads. It is like a pack of cards, each with a question on, being thrown at us. We certainly can't handle them all at once. In your diary/journal book turn to the back page and each time a question pops into your head, write it down. The process of attempting to answer these questions is slow and gradual. We may discover we find an answer, only to change our minds at a later date. There are no right and wrong answers, only answers you can identify with and find a sense of resolution for. You may want to look at the questions that you have written down over time. The questions that were important to you at first might now seem insignificant, with different issues now more important.

What question have you been thinking about today?

21 *Talk about the deceased*

If someone falls down and breaks their leg, they are rushed to hospital and have a plaster cast put on it. Everyone can see the injury and can give appropriate sympathy. Grief, however, goes unnoticed. After the initial support following a death and funeral, the world seems to rush on and no one seems to notice you. Even your closest friends don't know what to do. Sometimes people very close to you simply cannot cope with the loss and therefore seem to keep away from you. People are hesitant to talk to you about the deceased, as they think they will upset you and you may start to cry. What the world doesn't seem to realise is that you find yourself thinking about the deceased all the time. In fact, you think about them more now than when they were alive. This means we need plenty of opportunities to talk about the deceased. To use their name, to laugh and cry over your memories, to talk about what life is like without them and to toss about with questions relating to them. To do this we need friends who will be there for us and are willing to listen. This might mean accepting that your best friend is not the one to do this and you need to find others who will be able to give you what you need. People are often surprised at who becomes the best at supporting at times like this. Go with the flow, as your needs are now the most important. Seek out friends who will listen and be there for you and don't worry about those who can't cope and distance themselves from you. They are not your problem.

Who has helped you most on your grief journey?

22 *Call upon your past experience*

The loss you have experienced can seem like no other, especially if it was a very significant person in your life. You may feel you have no resources within you to cope with this experience. However, throughout life we encounter all sorts of losses. If you think back to your childhood experiences, perhaps you will recall going to school for the first time and being away from home. For many children this is their first experience of separation. We then change classes, teachers, perhaps move house etc. If you think through your life, you will see that there have been several occasions when you have experienced a loss and learned to cope with it. Although these losses are in no way as significant as the present loss, you do have experience to call upon to help you. Think about how you coped in the past and ask whether there was anything in those experiences that could help you to cope with this loss.

Draw a line on a piece of paper and write your age along the line at different points from 0 to your present age. Now mark any times in your life when you have experienced a loss. How did you cope?

23 *Laugh as well as cry*

We all express our emotions in our own personal way. Some of us find crying easy and can cry at the least little thing. Perhaps you can't watch a movie without shedding a tear at least once. Others find that they are dry as a bone and feel very uncomfortable if it seems that they might shed even one tear. We are all different and that's OK; be yourself. Funerals can often be where we are caught out. We often find we don't do as we expect at such events. There is no right or wrong way to behave at a funeral. Whether you cry or not, it doesn't reflect how you felt about the deceased. Some of us are 'all cried out' by the time of the funeral. Others find they don't cry until they are by themselves, when everyone has gone. Certainly, at some point we all need to express some emotion at our loss. Don't resist, as it can't harm. Sometimes we are like a can of pop that is 'all shook up'. Open it suddenly and you'll find you are in a mess. However, with gentle opening, we can let the gas out slowly. So feel free to cry as necessary. You might find yourself doing really well but suddenly something will trigger the emotional strings and you find yourself crying in the most unlikely places. This is very normal; you're not going mad. But remember also to laugh. You will have memories that you can share with others that bring a positive feeling to you. It's not disrespectful to the deceased to laugh and it can do you the world of good.

What was the funniest occasion you ever had with the deceased? Make sure a week doesn't go by without laughing at something, even if it is only at yourself.

24 *Stress, stress and more stress*

We all need a certain amount of pressure to help us meet deadlines and to keep us alert, but stress is something none of us need. Stress occurs when the pressure we experience is greater than the support to bear it. Imagine you have a thimble-sized cup in your brain. This cup holds emotions that you experience. If I drop a brick on your toe, you will feel pressure. We call it hurt or pain. The thimble cup fills up. Within a millisecond you might also feel another emotion, anger, and give me a dirty look or swear at me! Often, after anger we reflect and feel a little guilty. The cup is now filling with hurt, anger and guilt. If I come along with another brick, you will probably feel fearful. (I just might drop it again!) Hurt, anger, guilt, fear; no wonder the cup is almost full now with anxiety. When the cup is full, we are experiencing stress and it overflows as physical problems such as headaches, poor concentration, insomnia, loss of appetite or eating disorders. These are often the reasons we end up visiting the doctor. Now when you think about the death of someone close to you, perhaps you can see how your emotional cup has filled up. When people bump into you, emotion comes spilling out.

How full is your emotional cup?

What do you think is in it?

If you feel stressed, read No. 51 (Empty the can).

25 *Find an oasis*

'Have a break, have a . . .' says the advert. We all need to take breaks when situations get too much for us to bear. We are reminded about it on motorways when we read on the information signs, 'Tiredness kills, take a break.' There is the story of a mountain climber who was keen to reach the peak. He rushed up the hill, driving on porters who were carrying his baggage. After three days' climb, the porters refused to move. 'What's wrong?' demanded the mountaineer. 'We are waiting for our spirits to catch us up,' they explained. Many of us are like the mountaineer; we are always on the go, never stopping to rest or reflect. When we are bereaved, we may feel safer at home among familiar surroundings. But even at home, we can be busy bees always on the go, perhaps achieving little, yet with our minds racing. A change of environment may be a challenge to us when we feel vulnerable, but it can also be as good as a rest. You could make a spiritual retreat or simply pamper yourself. Perhaps you might like to go somewhere that was special to you in the past. Find a friend to go with you. You may find it easier to go away just for the day at first, then for a weekend or a few days, until you find your feet.

Decide to accept the next invitation that you receive.

Read No.100 and book a break away.

26 *Write lists*

When I was the rector of six county parishes spread over 60 square miles, I would find that I had endless answerphone messages always waiting for me. I don't know what I would have done without the answerphone and little sticky memory pads. By the end of a Sunday morning, parishioners had told me all sorts of information about the sick, where a person was in hospital, of meetings, and jobs to be done. The list was endless and if I had kept it all in my mind, I would have collapsed with exhaustion. However, by writing a list of the jobs and needs, I could unburden my mind and enjoy my Sunday roast.

When you are bereaved and your mind is working overtime, it is very easy to become absent-minded. By making a list you are releasing yourself from the pressure to remember. With any 'to do' list, begin by listing all the tasks. Then put them in order of priority. Make sure you put a simple task at the top of the list. This will encourage you when you achieve it. I always put a smiley face next to any task completed, as a way of making me feel good that I have succeeded in at least something. With big tasks, try and break them down into smaller jobs and see if there is anything on the list that you could delegate. It's always a good feeling when I complete the list and can tear it up.

Start today and make a short, simple list of achievable tasks. When you have a meeting with someone, write out what you want to say and don't be afraid to look at it in the meeting.

27 *People are annoying, accept it*

Yes, it is true – people are annoying! It is OK to admit the fact. They have the habit of coming out with all sorts of unhelpful comments:

'I understand what you are going though.' No, they don't!

'My loss was worse.' No, it wasn't!

'You're better off without him/her.' No, I'm not!

'They are in a better place now.' But surely the better place is with me!

'He/she was needed elsewhere.' But what about my needs?

People – aren't they a pain! But there is only one problem: aren't we people too? I guess we have also said inappropriate things at times. We do it because we feel embarrassed and want to make a situation better, only to find we have dug a hole to bury ourselves in. So give people a little slack, keep away from those who annoy you, forgive your family and friends, because despite their imperfections, we still need them, and one day they might need us.

Decide who empties your batteries and who charges the batteries up; then choose to spend time with the latter.

28 *Decide beforehand*

One of the biggest fears bereaved people have is how they are going to cope with the outside world. It all seems so unpredictable. We can't control how other people will react. Some will want to talk to you while others can't handle it, so will avoid you. There are those who know nothing about your loss while some find it all overwhelming. Some people want to smother you while others end up getting sympathy from you. The only thing you can control is yourself and even this is uncertain. We don't really know what we can cope with until we find ourselves encountering it. But we can do something to help. First, we can make sure we don't find ourselves being trapped. Position yourself near a door at meetings and conferences etc. so that when you have had enough, you can leave without a fuss. Secondly, think through a couple of responses that you will give to people when they ask you difficult questions. 'How's your husband/wife?', 'Are you married?', or 'How many children have you got?' will put you on the spot. There are no right or wrong answers, just ones that you are comfortable with. You will feel comfortable about talking openly with some people, while a short reply before walking on will be enough for others. Remember, how people react is not your responsibility; you must focus upon your own survival at this stage and allow others to find their own care support.

Sit down and write out in your journal what you will say if you meet someone in the supermarket who asks you:
'How is X (the deceased)?'
'How many children have you got?' (If a child has died.)
'How are you now?'
What other questions do you fear?

29 *Garden, cook, paint, dance . . .*

There are some things that are therapeutic, meaning simply that they are good for you. They include gardening, cooking, dancing, painting, reading poetry and listening to relaxing music. Choose to include a flavouring of these in your life and they will have a beneficial effect upon you. Gardening helps you to get fresh air and be in touch with nature. Cooking stimulates your taste buds and encourages you to be hospitable. Dancing of whatever kind allows you to lose yourself in your imagination and relaxes the body. Reading poetry releases the imagination and emotions. Painting allows you to express yourself and think 'outside the box'. Listening to music stimulates the emotions and can relax the body. You don't have to be knowledgeable or good at any of these things. Just fill each day with at least one of them and you will reap the benefit. You will find yourself smiling at things that once annoyed you, laughing at the ordinary things of life and feeling more content within yourself.

Why not sign up for a painting or dancing class, buy yourself a new plant or a piece of music or poetry book, or even start to write your own poetry?

30 *Beware of accidents*

Have you ever watched Ray Mears on television, talking about how to survive in the bush or jungle? He is amazing with all his skills. We don't live in the bush or the jungle but we have just as many skills to survive through difficult times. However, accidents still happen at the best of times. In fact, we are more likely to have an accident when we are under the weather, or recently bereaved or feeling depressed. This is because our minds are on other things, so our concentration is not as good as normal.

So follow the Boy Scout motto and 'be prepared'. The best way to do this is to first acknowledge we might be vulnerable to accidents. Secondly, take it easy on yourself by not doing too much or being in a hurry. Drive a little slower than normal; don't plan so much in a day's routine and give yourself space between tasks. In other words, look after yourself; no one else will.

Have you been more accident-prone lately?
What advice would you give another person
in this position?

31 Stop, look, listen

Can you recall being taught at school all about road safety? As a child, you were probably not that interested. But when you became a parent, suddenly it became important to drum into your children the simple refrain, 'Stop, look, listen, before crossing the road.' We know that when we stop listening, we become vulnerable to making the wrong decisions. When someone has died, we can find it difficult to listen and concentrate. This means we can easily make the wrong decisions. Family and friends can also seem to want us to get on with life and make decisions that we are not ready to face. 'Shall I dispose of the person's clothing?', 'What about all their possessions?', 'Shall I move house?' These are big decisions and only you can decide when you are ready. So go back to childhood and learn the lesson again. *Stop* – don't make rash decisions. You don't have to make any decisions in a rush. There is no need to deal with possessions until you are ready; they won't do any harm in the cupboard. *Look* – take your time. It can take months before a bereaved person can see the wood for the trees. *Listen* – hear what others are saying. Find out what they really want you to do and, more importantly, why. Often their reasons are because they want you to feel better. If following their advice won't help you, then you need to say so. Call and rely upon your own intuition. In the end, you know best. Decisions made in haste are often regretted. And remember, if you can't be bothered to read the small print, then don't sign.

Do you feel under pressure to make major decisions? What decisions seem small to your family or friends but seem large to you?

32 *I don't do finance*

Everybody has to deal with finance sooner or later. Yet it can seem the last thing to bother with when someone has died. However, eventually it will have an impact upon you. You may find yourself very worried about your finances in your new position. Will you have enough to live on? Do other people now have a claim upon your finances and possessions? It is very natural to want to bury your head in the sand and just hope it all goes away. Alas, it will not. However, if you deal with it, in the end you will become more relaxed and may even feel pleased with yourself for sorting it out. The good news is that you are not alone. Find someone you trust to look into your situation. You may also need an independent financial advisor to talk through your situation. Choose someone who is recommended (beware of leaflets through the door), is accredited and has no other interest in your financial situation, i.e. does not represent anyone else who will benefit from the inheritance. That's why it is good to have two independent people to look into the situation. Too many people have been robbed by so-called professional friends. An extra pair of eyes will safeguard your future.

Take your time; ask around before coming to a decision about who to ask for advice.

Key times

33 *Anniversaries*

There are specific times in the year that bereaved people often dread. These might be a birthday, when the person died, the date of the coroner's report, a wedding anniversary, etc. We are unsure how we will be on the day and fear the worst. But often the fear of the day that is looming can be worse than the actual day. Rather than trying not to think about the day, it is easier to plan the day so that you have some control over it. This might mean taking the day off work, going out for the day, taking flowers to the grave; spending time with people you feel secure and relaxed with, going to a favourite place of the deceased, or doing something that the deceased loved to do. Whatever you do, by planning the day, you reduce the fear of the unknown.

In your journal, write down key dates that are significant to you and which you know will be difficult to handle.

34 *Christmas*

Christmas is a hard time to cope with, when all you want to do is bypass it and get to January. It is hard to think about preparations without the deceased. Buying presents for family and friends is also difficult because you can feel guilty, as it can seem you are diminishing the importance of the deceased. The answer lies in forward-planning. Decide early on where you will spend Christmas, before you are asked and put in a difficult position. You don't want to spend Christmas where you would rather not be. If buying presents is difficult for you, why not simply give money or vouchers for one year? It won't do any harm and people will understand. To remember the deceased, why not buy a present first for them before you buy any others for your family? This might seem strange but it can be liberating, freeing you from guilt to get on with Christmas. The present might simply be a plant or a donation to charity. Having recognised the deceased, you can then focus upon others. On the big day make life simple for yourself. Let others do the cooking, and when invited out, let the friends or relatives know that you might only stay for a short while. This allows you to make a quick escape if at any point you feel trapped. What about the duty of Christmas cards? If you are brave enough, just don't send any in the first year; it won't do any harm. If you can afford it, get a printed card produced so that all you have to do is write the envelopes; or a cheaper way is to print a short, standard note, which you pop into each card. But remember, don't let duty weigh you down.

Write down what you feel you can cope with, what you definitely don't want for Christmas and build upon the positive.

35 *Holidays*

We all look forward to holidays but they don't always turn out as planned at the best of times. It is even more complex for those who are bereaved. First, you just don't want to go away, even though everyone is telling you that this is what you need. Secondly, planning a holiday should be a cheerful thing that you enjoy, but when you feel drained each day, the effect seems too much bother. Thirdly, going away can make you feel that you are betraying the deceased by leaving them. So what's the answer? Begin with small trips away, nothing complicated, where you can come back home quickly and easily. Only when you have become acquainted with leaving the house and locality, begin to think about a longer holiday. Make sure the people you travel with understand what you are going through and will give you the space you require when needed. Many people find it helpful to visit the grave or a special place of memory to acknowledge the deceased before going away. By thinking, talking and acknowledging, we can give ourselves permission to take our leave. For some, visiting old holiday places where you went with the deceased can be very comforting. It allows you to remember, to laugh, to cry and to move on. For others, some kind of structure to the holiday can help to fill the gap. Perhaps learning a new craft or skill with a friend will prove to be very beneficial.

Think of whom you could spend time away with.
Could they do the organising?

36 Birthdays

Birthdays are but once a year yet they feel as if they come around all too quickly. Whether it's your birthday or the birthday of the deceased, it can be a sensitive time. Rather than just dread the day, choose to think creatively. If you know it is going to be difficult for you, then book the day off work. Remember, the fear of an unorganised day is far worse than the day itself. See it as a day to treat yourself. Book yourself into a spa and pamper yourself. Organise a day out with a friend. Because it is hard to know just how you will be feeling, it is better to let others do the cooking, driving etc. Choose to do something positive on the birthday of the deceased. Go and work in a charity shop for the day or give a small gift to a favoured charity. If you are religious, visit a holy place or spend a day in a retreat centre (see No. 100). Whatever you do, don't let the day control you; you control the day. It will be far less exhausting in the end.

Look at the calendar and begin to plan the day.
Who would you like to spend it with?
Where would you like to go?

37 *Routines*

Why should I give myself special times to think about my loss when, in fact, I'm thinking about it all of the time? Well, eventually we do need to be able to concentrate on other matters. But we can feel as if we are betraying the deceased by not thinking of them. So if we set aside a time each day to reflect and focus upon issues relating to the deceased, it can then free us to focus upon other tasks for the day. This works particularly well if we choose to go to see a counsellor. By talking to someone else once a week, we know we will be focusing upon our loss in a concentrated way. This then allows us to put all the questions and issues to one side during the week, until we see the counsellor again. I often imagine it is like having a locked box where I put all the things that worry me. I can turn the key and lock the box, knowing that I don't have to think about them all week, as they are now safe. When I see my counsellor, I can turn the key and open the box and together begin to deal with the issues that have arisen during that week. It doesn't have to be a counsellor that I see but someone I know I can chat to, who will listen to me without judgement. Routines are made to release us from having to worry every second of the day, so don't fight them, flow with them.

Are there things that you worry about which could be put aside to be dealt with at a set time?
Write down in your journal issues that arise each day. Then set a time and place to focus upon them with a friend, relative or counsellor.

38 *A place to visit*

If the deceased has been buried, then visiting the grave can be a great comfort. It is an opportunity for you to have a few minutes focusing upon the deceased. Taking flowers, tidying the grass around the grave, organising a gravestone and having a few private moments to talk to the deceased can help in releasing the pressure within. Some believe that we never truly relinquish the bond with the deceased; we simply find a way of accommodating them within our lives as we move forward. We thus carry the loved one with us. By giving special times to focus upon the deceased, it can then release us to get on with the daily chores of life. Where burial has not taken place, then it could be where we have located the ashes. It is not unusual to delay in dealing with the ashes for months or years. But if you can find somewhere that is a special place for you, then it can be very constructive as it gives you direction to focus your thoughts and memories at special times. Remember that if you choose to bury ashes within your garden, it can then be very difficult to ever move from that house. For others, the planting of trees, rose-bushes, flowers, or placing a park bench in a special place etc., can provide us with that sacred location where we can be alone with our special thoughts and memories. If you don't have a special location, then find a thinking spot that is special to you.

Do you still need to organise a gravestone
or the disposal of the ashes?
Is there a space that you could develop with flowers etc.
that could be a blessing to you as well as others?

Memories

39 *Memory jar*

You will need a small glass jar, a bag of salt – enough to fill the jar, some coloured chalks and some newspaper. Think about five or six special memories that you have of the deceased. It may be special times, events, places or activities. Divide the salt into the number of memories. Choose a colour for each memory and rub the chalk over the salt until it becomes the colour you want it to be. Now pour it into the jar. Repeat the exercise until the jar is full to the brim. (This is important, otherwise the salt will all get mixed together.) Seal the top. Make a chart of what the different colours represent. This can be stuck to the side of the glass jar.

Put the jar in a place that you find a comfort to you. Use the jar to remind you regularly of your special memories.

Talk to someone about what each coloured layer means to you. This is a useful exercise to do with a relative or friend.

40 *Memory box*

When someone has died, the bereaved often go through a period of not being able to recall the deceased clearly. It can sometimes be difficult to picture the deceased. There is a fear that you might not be able to hold on to precious thoughts and memories. What can be helpful is to make a memory box. This consists of a box such as a shoebox or something more special. Think of what you could put into the box that would help you remember the deceased. This could be photographs, jewellery such as a watch or a ring, a special memento, notes, diaries, poems, CDs, pressed flowers, the order of service from the funeral or anything else that is special to you and helps you remember. By gathering these things together, it releases you from having to hold on to these memories. You can get the box out any-time you want, to reflect upon special memories, and then place the box back into a safe place.

What could you put in the box?

How would you decorate the outside?

41 *Press a flower*

There are times when you simply don't want to do anything at all. The letters keep arriving, bills build up and there is correspondence to sort out. At times like this, do something that feels as if it will be a comfort to you; something that will make you feel a little closer to the deceased. Think of the flowers that were bought at the time of the funeral. There may have been specially selected flowers that the deceased loved or that reminded you of a special occasion. Why not go and get a flower that will remind you of the deceased and choose to have it pressed. This gives you something with a purpose to do, that will result in you having something that can be a focus, even if it is only for a few moments now and again.

Can you recall what flowers were at the funeral? You may have been in a daze at the funeral and now can't recall. Ask a relative or friend what they remember. Each week get some flowers for the house that remind you.

42 Music and bubble bath

In our grief we can find that our mind is racing and always on the go. The wrong kind of noise fills our day, leaving us feeling mentally and physically exhausted. But there are other noises that perhaps we once enjoyed that have been pushed to the periphery. In spring and summer: the sound of buzzing bees and the singing of the birds. In autumn: the sound of the wind rustling the leaves and shaking the branches. In winter: the patter of the rain and the crispness of the frost. We all need time to get back in touch with nature; to go and hear the sea whistle in our ears as our feet crunch the pebbles. There is something magical about nature that helps to restore our equilibrium. And when we can't get outside, then bring the outside in. Have a warm bubble bath as you listen to some relaxing music. There is such a range of music available today that focuses upon helping to relax the mind and body. Another remedy is to join a choir or simply attend a church service. Music and singing is very therapeutic as it releases the emotions and lifts you to a higher plane.

This week, treat yourself to a new piece of music and some sweet-smelling bubble bath.

43 *Listen to the echo*

When we are in the midst of grief, it can seem that a thick fog surrounds our lives. It hovers around us wherever we go. This clouds two things. First, our vision of the way ahead is confused. It is very difficult to move on with life when there is a large portion of you wanting to linger in the past. We want to hold on to our memories for fear of losing them and in any case, 'How can we possibly move forward without our loved one?' It all seems unfair. This is why it is often best not to make big decisions early in your loss. If you can wait, it will allow you to see the wood for the trees. Secondly, this fog clouds our hearing. Our mind is actively 24/7 thinking and processing what has happened to us. This means you will find people speaking to you, or having conversations that just seem to pass you by. Don't panic, you're not going mad or deaf. It just means you are not ready yet for new detail to enter your life. That is why it is better to engage with people in small doses where you can concentrate on what is being said. In time, you will find your memory and concentration will return to you. If you have important meetings coming up, try and write down any questions you might have about the subject. Writing down the answers people give you can allow you to think through the meeting at a later date. It can be helpful to have another person with you so that they can be your eyes and ears.

When you find you are not listening to a person, it is because you are concentrating on something else that is important to you. Try writing down your thoughts so that you can make sense of them. Is there someone you could talk to about them?

44 *Read in the spirit*

When something happens to us that we don't understand, it is natural that we search for answers. Reading books can be one way of helping on the journey of the search. There are a great number of books out there that might help you to formulate your own conclusions. Some are practical, others psychological, while many are stories of people's experiences. We can find a comfort in discovering we are not the only ones walking this way. Allow reading to become a catalyst for you to express your thoughts. Do you agree with what you read? Has the book missed the mark? Does the book make you feel angry? Why? Could you do better? Perhaps you might think about writing up your journal. It doesn't matter if you don't publish it, simply writing it would be beneficial to you. Some people have different books on the go all at the same time. Scatter them around the house. Pick them up and put them down. You don't have to complete them. Bit by bit, thought by thought, what goes into your thoughts and how you process them will help you put together this jigsaw of your life.

Why not spend an hour looking at what relates to you in a bookshop?

Difficult issues

45 Dealing with possessions

One of the hardest things to handle when a death has occurred is deciding what to do with the possessions and belongings of the deceased. A natural tendency of people is to think it is better to tidy up and sort out everything as quickly as possible, to allow the bereaved to get on with their lives. There's only one problem. That, for many bereaved people, is the last thing they want to do. By getting rid of possessions, you can feel as if you are disposing of the deceased. People can feel comforted by the belongings of the deceased. They are objects that have always been around you, they have a characteristic smell that connects you with the deceased and they can help in recalling special memories. So don't feel pressurised in dealing with items until you feel able to handle them. For some, it is too upsetting to see familiar objects around the house and they are, therefore, happy to remove items. Others need to place items somewhere safe and special, until they decide what they will do with them. There is no perfect timing in dealing with possessions. Some things are just too precious and you will hold on to them all your life. With other items, you will eventually wonder why you are holding on to them, and feel comfortable about removing them. Many take belongings to charity shops, knowing at least someone else will use the clothes etc.

Don't be rushed, do things in your own time. You, more than anyone, will know the right time to deal with the possessions.

Are there some things I want to keep and others I could release?

Is there somewhere I could put the belongings so that I can deal with them in my time?

46 *Aloneness*

When the dust settles, families have returned home, people have gone back to work and to their normal routine, we are finally left alone. At first, adrenalin, things to do and people around you keep you going. But now, finally, you have to come down to earth with a bang. As the world rushes on, you can feel left behind, with no one noticing you or appearing to care. This sense of loneliness and desolation can be the worst period of grief. You can now feel a distance from the deceased with little to look forward to in the future. It is a time of solace. Some days you wake and the sun is shining and you feel like getting on with life. But other days you awake to grey clouds and a sense of heaviness. All of this is very normal. Go easy on yourself. You have little control over the weather and, at first, you can feel the same way about your feelings. But slowly and gradually, just as the seasons creep up on us, we find ourselves progressing. Until then, take each day at a time. On good days be busy; on bad days take it easy, and in the darkest of days, keep telling yourself that tomorrow will be different. Remember, you are allowed difficult times in your life. It is a sign of your love and commitment to the deceased.

When the difficult days come, know what works best for you. Are you better alone or with a friend? How could you treat yourself? Remember, you don't have to deal with all your problems on one day.

47 Suicidal thoughts

Suicidal thoughts are frightening, but very common. It is like being at the top of a building looking down; there seems to be a weight pulling you in the wrong way. Such thoughts arrive at our door for several reasons. First, the pain that we feel can seem just too great. Secondly, we have this longing to be with the deceased. Thirdly, we can feel isolated, thinking no one understands us. Fourthly, there seems little to look forward to in the future. These four things can't be magically removed, but if we break them down, one by one they can be dealt with. The pain, which is very real and physical, will eventually go. The doctor could reassure you. Secondly, the longing is a sign of your attachment to the deceased. Grief is as much about holding on, as it is about losing. What would the deceased want for your life now? Try focusing on what you had. The more thankful you are for your memories, the more you can come to terms with them. Thirdly, although we feel alone, we don't have to be. Often people just don't know how you are feeling. If a friend or relative does not seem to understand, then find someone who can. The doctor could refer you to a bereavement counsellor or you could contact one of a variety of support agencies. Cruse, the bereavement support agency, will have a group near you. Finally, the future may well feel bleak, but be assured spring and summer always follow winter. Hold on to that fact.

Is there someone you could talk to about your feelings? Is there something positive you could do in memory of the deceased? Can you book something for the future that you know would be good for you?

48 Facing our thoughts

In the midst of grief, there seem more things to think about every day. They may revolve around events of the past, or how the person died. Thoughts might be focusing on the probate, financial matters and general fears for the future. Whatever our thoughts linger upon, eventually we have to take control of them. Some thoughts are time limited and practical. They might relate to the Will, sorting out paperwork or handling the possessions. Other thoughts relate to events of the past, as you try and make sense of it all. If there are factual issues that you are unclear about (e.g. how or why the deceased died), then it can help to go and obtain additional information to allow you to come to a conclusion about the past. Other thoughts can be less specific and harder to unravel. It can help to write them down. Do they have any common theme? Are they thoughts that you could share with another? Do the thoughts look less of an issue now that you have written them down? If you find your thoughts are just going round and round in your head like a tape recording, write them out and make a list of possible answers. The sooner we come to a satisfactory conclusion, the sooner we will be able to move on.

Why do you feel you are thinking about this issue?
Why is it important to you?
Do you lack the information to make a conclusion?
Is there something you haven't accepted?

49 *Facing our fears*

We all experience fears in our lives. Normally we are able to control them, but when we are bereaved sometimes the fears seem to overwhelm us. They can cause physical symptoms such as panic attacks with our hearts pounding, our skin sweating and our stomach feeling sick. At times it can seem that the fear never leaves us. Short-term answers may be tranquillisers from the doctor or herbal tranquillisers, which are not addictive. Herbal teas can also help. Doing a relaxation exercise can help, but in the end we have to face our fears. This means taking our fears apart, bit by bit and looking at them long enough to understand them. This is not a quick process and needs time. A friend or therapist can help you look at your fears. Worrying never solves anything; in fact, it only makes matters worse. Ask yourself, 'Will I worry about this next year, in three years' time, or even on my deathbed?' At first you might say 'yes', but on further thinking, we often decide it is not something we'll remember in years to come. Remind yourself of other fears in your early life that you have overcome and hardly remember.

It is helpful to note down when we particularly sense the fear. What causes it? Is there something we can do about it? Write down the alternative outcomes. Give yourself time limits to think about a fearful issue. When the time is up, make yourself go off and do something constructive.

50 *Half-time – time out*

Many sporting events have a half-time. It allows the players to catch up with themselves, giving their bodies time to recover and their minds to reassess. So, have a little nap; you have done well in getting this far. You are halfway on your journey of grief. Give yourself a treat for staying the course. The journey of grief is often longer than we expect. Our society seems to want bereaved people to be back to normal as quickly as possible. This is human nature's own protection mechanism. If we see that the bereaved are coping, then perhaps we will cope when it happens to us. Work places can be lenient at first but eventually they want their worker to be putting in a full day's work. Alas, for many the road of grief is an arduous journey with many ups and downs. This means you have to take the long view. There is no quick fix when your loved one dies. All you can do is adjust to the situation and find a way forward. Grief can seem rather like a pendulum. There are times when you focus intensely upon your loss, but you can't stay like that all of the time. We need to swing the other way and focus upon the routine, normal things of life. Part of this is to look after yourself, even when you can't be bothered. So go easy on yourself and have a break.

What can you do or organise that would be a real tonic to you? Who can you share this with?

Emotions

51 *Empty the can*

We have talked about how we can feel like a can of pop, all 'shook up' and about to explode, and how our emotional cup can seem very full, ready to spill over at any time. We can't function very well with a full cup. It is never empty but we can seek to keep it half-full. Some people try and empty the cup with physical exercise, others prefer to switch off by watching TV, or smoking or drinking. Others prefer socialising and talking to friends. Some methods of de-stressing are better than others. Generally, hurt needs to be acknowledged, anger needs to be expressed in a controlled way, guilt needs a listening ear and to find forgiveness. Fear needs to be rationalised and understood. It is only then that anxiety and stress diminish.

In your diary or dream-book draw a cup or can. Fill the vessel up with the words of hurt, anger, guilt, fear, anxiety and stress. Next to these words write or draw what makes you feel like this. Can you identify any physical problems coming out of the vessel? Perhaps you have been to see the doctor about them. What do you think would empty some of this emotion in the cup or can? Write down what comes to you.

52 *Guilt and more guilt*

Everyone feels guilty at some time or other in life. But when someone dies, there can seem to be so many things to be guilty about: events of the past or questions of whether you did enough. Enjoying yourself and just being alive can be enough to bring on guilty feelings. Mostly we feel guilt without being guilty. For many of us, guilt pangs can leave us feeling emotionally paralysed. Perhaps this is why we so often try and bury our feelings, if they are submerged, we can't see them. Unfortunately, we can't bury guilt deep enough to get rid of it. Sooner or later it will come to the surface as anger or depression. It can diminish our self-esteem and cause us to hide away. The answer lies in acknowledging the guilt, whether it is justified or not. It is only by bringing it out into the open that others can help us see the wood for the trees. We can then see the guilt for what it is and allow others to help us find a way of resolving it.

True guilt can be removed by acknowledgement and forgiveness. False guilt needs to be shown up for what it is and dismissed.

Try writing down what you feel guilty about. Now ask yourself what the deceased would say about each situation. Would they forgive you? Can you choose to forgive yourself? Find a friend that you trust to share this with and get their perspective on the situation. Perhaps a local minister of religion could help you work through your feelings and bring absolution, if necessary, on behalf of God and the deceased.

53 *It's OK to love and be angry*

There are times and situations that just make your blood boil with rage and anger. It's as natural as eating or sleeping. We can be angry with the deceased, ourselves, God, the medical profession, and even those around us who are trying to help us. Life is just not fair and it is only right that we feel angry about death and our situation. There is not a lot we can do about this emotion, except acknowledge it and find a way of handling it so that it doesn't harm others or ourselves. If we turn the anger inwards to ourselves then we will just compound the situation. Anger is best turned outwards. If we are angry with God, then surely he already knows about it. Why not tell him your feelings; I think he will appreciate your honesty. If you are angry about the deceased, try writing a letter to them expressing what you feel. You may not be able to post it, but it will help you work through the feelings. If you are angry with other people, then think about how you can tell them in a controlled way, acknowledging that there are also a lot of things you love and like about them. By asking why the other person behaved the way they did, we can get a better perspective on the situation. Remember, we can still love a person even though we are angry with them.

Expressing anger in a safe way can change how you feel. Try punching a cushion or kicking leaves in the garden. If the anger is getting too much for you, count to ten, breathe deeply, walk away from the scene, or hunch your shoulders and then let them relax to release the tension within.

54 *Handling the lion*

When you go through the experience of grief you will have different emotions: numbness, disbelief, hurt, anger, guilt, fear and every other emotion in the book. We keep some of these emotions hidden away under lock and key, while others come bursting out of us at times we least expect. The one emotion that can do the most damage is anger. We need to find a way of handling this emotion so that it doesn't remain trapped within us, yet doesn't hurt others or ourselves when it comes out. There are different ways of expressing this feeling. Draw a picture of how you are feeling. Make a paper aeroplane and write all over it what makes you feel angry. Then throw it as hard as you can. Get a ball of clay and keep working it into a shape. When complete, destroy it and start again. Have a shower when no one else is in the house and let your feelings out, nice and loud. Write down everything that frustrates you and then burn the list. Gardening can be an effective way of working through your anger as you dig and turn, dig and turn.

If the anger is deep-seated, perhaps you need to see a counsellor to change the way you think, act or react.

55 *Panic attacks*

Panic attacks occur when we feel that we just can't cope with what is ahead of us. Our bodies go through such a lot when adrenalin is pumped through our veins, telling us that it is all too much to bear. Suddenly the weight that we bear seems beyond what we can carry. When this occurs we need to follow a clear procedure. This involves turning the stress into action. Simply punching a cushion can release stressful energy. Practise a calming exercise. Breathe deeply and slowly (if you are hyperventilating breathe into a brown paper bag). Tense your muscles one by one, working from the head to the toes and then gradually release them.

Calmly, imagine a very happy memory in your life. Try and picture the detail of the scene, hear the noises and smell the atmosphere. Stay with this picture for a few minutes. Now do the same with a memory of when you were very confident and everything went well. Now think of a time when you have had a panic attack and think at the same time of the happy scene and successful scene. Pull these pictures together so that when you think about the difficult situation you can see yourself succeeding and feeling confident. This takes a little practice, but it is effective.

56 *We all have fears*

The future without the deceased can seem very daunting. It can make us withdraw and not want to face the future. We can also feel we are betraying the deceased by moving on without them. There can also be the longing to go and be with the deceased, even if this means leaving others behind. Suicidal thoughts are not unusual for those in grief. Often, being able to talk about these mixed feelings is enough to release the pressure felt within. We need to reach into the resources that we have used in the past. If we look back over our lives we will see that we have encountered many types of losses in life. The first day at school away from home, moving class, school or house, leaving school for college or for your first job. Throughout life we experience moments of loss. What has helped you through these changes?

Draw a timeline of all of the changes in your life. Remind yourself how you have coped and adapted. Also draw upon the wishes of the deceased and how they would have wanted you to overcome this difficult period.

57 *Depression*

I suspect we all experience depression at some time in our lives. There are different levels of depression. Many people can get better on their own, but others find themselves being pulled down into confusion and hopelessness. Doctors regard this as an illness and may treat it with drugs or with a talking therapy. Depression is not new, Hippocrates described it in 400BC and it can be found in almost all cultures. So if you feel this applies to you, don't think you are on your own. Winston Churchill, Beethoven, Darwin, Tolstoy, and many comedians have preceded you. Symptoms of depression might include mood swings, poor concentration, indecision, lack of appetite, and sleeplessness. In bereavement, your doctor might call it 'reactive depression'. This is a result of pain, hurt, anger, guilt, and finally despair building up within you. The past seems too painful and the future too fearful to contemplate. If we are feeling like this we need to be kind to ourselves.

Be realistic; it takes time to overcome depression and loss. Don't deny what is happening to you. The sooner we face our situation, the sooner we can find answers. Make sure you get plenty of rest, fluids and fresh air. You may not have a plaster cast on your leg but you need just as much care. Seek out people who make you feel good and have a break from anything that pulls you down. Finally, find a doctor who is sympathetic to you and will journey with you out of the mire.

58 *Dealing with your thoughts*

When grief strikes, the mind is bombarded with many thoughts. There are many memories of the past, confusion over what to do now and all sorts of fears for the future.

We need to try and control our thinking so that our stress levels are controlled. The simpler we keep our daily routine, so that we are focusing upon one thing at a time, the more we will be able to cope. When we are low, it is easy to fall into negative thinking. 'If only he hadn't died.', 'I should have been there.' or 'I can't cope now.' It can be hard to identify negative thinking, especially if we have had a lifetime of tending to think in that way. We all have a tendency to play familiar tapes over and over in our mind. But we can change the tapes if we want to. It may take time, but by telling ourselves that we are OK, we are good enough, and we will survive, we can slowly begin to change our mindset.

Try monitoring how you think throughout the day. Write down an event of the day, then what you thought and felt. Finally write down what you think after a few hours and try to correct your thinking. If you can identify what you are telling yourself, it can be the beginning of changing your attitude.

Search for meaning

59 *So many questions*

When a major tragedy occurs in our lives, it is inevitable that we find ourselves reassessing our belief system. There are just so many questions that require answers.

Even questions which we thought we had answered in life, need to be reappraised.

It is not uncommon for the bereaved to begin to think about moving house or changing careers. Those who have a religious belief may find themselves wondering whether they believe in God in the same way; while people who did not believe in God, might find themselves wondering if there is life after death after all. Don't panic, it is very normal and natural to begin to think in new ways about your belief. It can be a long journey of self-discovery as you reflect upon your experience. Be patient with yourself and accept that you don't have to have life all worked out.

Give yourself time before you make big decisions. Write a journal of your thoughts, the things you want to change and what you believe. It is only as we look back that we can see clearly how we have changed.

60 *Look for answers*

Where do I find the answers to the questions that are haunting me? Well, it will depend on what the questions are. The bereaved often have issues relating to the illness, accident or how the person died. Hopefully you will find that the local authorities, whether the doctor, police or fire brigade, are helpful. It is important to find out all the facts so that you can make sense of what has happened to you. Other questions may require friends to bounce off ideas about the future, what to do with the belongings, whether to go on holiday, or the much bigger question about life after death. A local minister of religion should be skilled enough to assist you on your search without giving you platitudes or quick-fix answers. The bereaved often find that reading related topics can be of great assistance in their search for answers. There is a large volume of books available, many written by the bereaved expressing their own journey. It is often as we look at other people's stories that we find answers for ourselves.

There are often support groups in existence that relate to your loss. If you join such a group you will meet others who are asking the same questions. It is easier to find answers with others than just by yourself.

61 Heaven?

Whatever your belief system may be, when we encounter death, it is natural to wonder what has happened to our loved ones. Those who believe there is no afterlife may find comfort in recognising that the elements from the deceased are still alive, with the neutrons and protons within the atoms still circling as fast as ever and continuing to play their part within the universe. Others will look for answers in religion. I have met many people who, after a tragic loss, have held on to their faith, albeit having adjusted how they perceive God. Perhaps God becomes less of a genie who just gives you what you want, or their attitude to prayer changes. Others hold on to their belief while finding organised religion difficult to handle. It is also not unusual to say you don't believe in God while still praying to him for your loved ones. After all, it is normal to be angry with God or feel let down by him when a disaster occurs.

Whatever our background, we can still find comfort and reflection by reading passages that relate to the afterlife. The Bible has a number of verses that can help us in our thinking.

Trying reading a particular passage and reflect upon it for the day. Possible verses may include:

Deuteronomy 33:27
Psalm 23
Psalm 147:3-5
Matthew 28:20
Mark 10:14b-16
Luke 23:43
John 3:16
John 11:31-36
John 14:1-6
Romans 8:35-39
1 Corinthians 2:9
1 Corinthians 15:20-28
1 Corinthians 15:35-46
1 Corinthians 15:51-57
2 Corinthians 1:3-7
Philippians 1:21-23
1 Thessalonians 4:13-18
1 Peter 1:3, 4
Revelation 7:13-17
Revelation 21:1-7

62 *Assumptions*

One day I was standing in my lounge when I heard a crack. It was the ceiling collapsing, which demolished my lounge. I spend the next six months very conscious of the ceiling in every room I went into. I behaved in a similar way when my house was burgled. I was suddenly conscious of any movement outside the house. My assumptive world had been shattered. I had assumed that ceilings do not move and that my house was safe. We all live our lives according to a whole range of community rules and personal rules. This leads us to a set of assumptions, which give us confidence to live our lives. We assume that if we obey the rules we will be rewarded with a fulfilling life. However, when a loved one dies, even if expected, our assumptions are often broken. Bad things do happen to good people. We can easily feel we must have done something wrong to be punished in this way. Alas, it is just one of those circumstances of life.

Reflect for a moment on the many disasters that have happened over the past few years. Train crashes, bombs in the underground, gas explosions and many more. Think about whether the people involved in these situations were to blame. So many innocent people are just in the wrong place, at the wrong time. Are you one of these people?

63 *Stillness*

In our search for answers we need to find a special place, an oasis, to allow ourselves to refresh our bodies and find the space to reflect. We all need time to relax deeply and to find a higher transcendent state. It's a state of mind, which is neither low with fears nor high with hopes. Special, solace places allow us to look within and to acknowledge who and where we are. It is recognised that a healthy spiritual life contributes to one's state of mind. Prayer, meditation and contemplation can be very rewarding. You don't have to be religious to reap the benefits. Prayer allows us to engage in a two-way process as we commune with God and allow ourselves to be open to his thoughts. Meditation is when we focus upon a piece of scripture, or words of wisdom or perhaps a poem, which we then reflect upon for minutes, hours or days. Contemplation is when we sit in silence repeating just a word or a phrase such as 'Maranatha' (Come, Lord Jesus), or 'Lord Jesus Christ, have mercy upon me.', or 'Be still and know that I am God'. By planning a day away from the ordinary, we are telling ourselves that we are still special and worthy, even if we don't feel like it.

Plan ahead and book two or three individual days away. This might be to a place with fond memories, to the coast or countryside, or perhaps to a leisure centre or retreat house. If you are unsure what to do, try an organised retreat, as this will provide a little direction whilst still having plenty of space for yourself in a safe environment. The national retreat details are at the back of the book *(see No. 100).*

64 *Science and atoms*

For those who are not religious and have no belief of the afterlife, there needs to be a way of making sense of it all without being left with nothing but emptiness. One approach is to see that the deceased has completed their life rather like a book. There are large books with many pages while other books are small and succinct. Both types of book are complete with introductions and conclusions. The book is finished and that is the end of the matter. Another approach is to see that the deceased consisted of many elements of life. These elements still exist. The atoms with their protons, neutrons and electrons are still continuing to dance in formation. They are still perfectly formed and will go on existing for eternity. Others find it helpful to get involved in an organisation which is fighting the disease or trying to prevent the cause of death. This can contribute to a sense of purpose and understanding surrounding our loss.

Think about contributing to something that will have long-term effects. This could be planting a tree, making a donation to a special cause, or assisting a local charity.

65 *Attitude is important*

We choose our attitude of life. Our character, our upbringing and our belief system affect this. What we do know is that our mind can affect many parts of our body's system. It is not uncommon for the bereaved to have a lower immune system and be vulnerable to infections. But in the end, we can choose our attitude and state of mind. We can exist as if the sword of Damacles is hanging over us by a single hair's breadth as we wait for more disasters to occur. Or we can decide, little by little, to turn the corner and look for positives in life. Beginning to eat a little better or getting more fresh air can make a big difference. Small positive attitudes eventually lead to a more permanent healthy state of mind. Beware of your emotions swinging from negative to very positive. Being overelated can be as harmful as being very negative. Look for small increments of change, aiming to find an equilibrium that is right for yourself.

Reading back into a diary can show you how far you have travelled. Try writing down a list of positive things you might like to achieve, however small they may be.

66 *Altruism*

Although nothing can ever compensate for the death of a person, nevertheless good things can result. One of the best outcomes of bereaved people is that they can begin to understand other people's problems and become more sympathetic. Many charities have been formed because of another person's loss. They go on to bring joy and healing to people's lives, yet the catalyst was the death of an individual. Bereaved people often become less materialistic, suffer fools less gladly, choose not to waste time, and spend their lives with people who understand. All of this contributes to our community and society. The loss is never far away, but bereaved people go on to do things that would make the deceased very proud.

I wonder what you might be able to go on to achieve?

67 *Read and decide*

There are now many books written by the bereaved. It can be very therapeutic to write about your experience, regardless of whether it is published. When grieving, it is natural to want to look for answers. As we read about other people's experiences, it can allow us to think afresh about our story and to rethink what we believe. We will find books that annoy and enrage us, while others will affirm our experience. It is less important whether we like the books written about grief or not; what is key is that they engage us in working through our own thought processes so that we can begin to make sense of it all. Remember, it is the bereaved who are the experts on this subject. Just as a book may be helpful to you, you in turn may one day be very helpful to another bereaved person.

The bereavement support agencies such as Cruse or Compassionate Friends have a good book list to guide the bereaved. Details are at the back of the book (No. 101).

Finding direction

68 *Quash those fears*

There are many fears when a loved one dies. Fears about oneself, facing the future, finance, family, health and many more. Fear affects some more than others but we all experience it. It can hang over us, as if each moment of the day is packed with an unknown waiting to hit us. This can be terribly debilitating. It can affect us physically with upset stomachs, headaches and panic attacks, and prevent us from making the simplest of decisions. As a way of coping, we can pull the blind down on our fear so that we don't have to analyse and deal with it. But eventually we do have to face our fears. We need a strategy that will help us move forward. First, see if you can write down your fears. Secondly, when they occur try and limit the time you are going to think about them. This is not easy but with practice it does work. Thirdly, reduce the fear down to size. Imagine something much larger coming to swallow the fear up. Make the picture in your mind funny and positive. Fourthly, remember how you overcame a similar fear in the past. Finally, tell another person. It is remarkable how often by just talking about it, the fear seems to diminish.

Make a decision that it is time to tackle your fears. Work through these five points and see what difference it makes.

69 *Decisions*

Try and make decisions when you are not feeling at a low ebb or when you feel high. Make a list of good effects and a list of negative results. What do those who love you want? What do you want? What will you feel years later about this decision? Imagine you are moving house and stay with the feelings for a good hour. Does this bring a mood of light simplicity? Try thinking the opposite: how does this feel? If the answer is unclear, it is not the time to make the decision. Remember, many decisions in life are often not right or wrong. You simply have to find an answer which fits you most comfortably. That might not be what your friends would choose but what feels right to you. However, that doesn't stop you from sharing with friends and family. It's hard to find answers in isolation. We all need a sounding-board to help us along the way.

Make a list of decisions that you feel you have to make and put them in categories of urgent, this week, this month, and eventually. Now tackle one decision at a time. Treat yourself with something positive when you have made a decision.

70 *Enjoy without forgetting*

Being bereaved is like wearing a second skin. Other people might not be aware of it but you know that this extra layer goes with you everywhere. You can choose to make this a positive thing, knowing that your loved one is close to you and is still influencing your life. (If you had a very negative experience with the deceased, refer to No. 82.)

Don't let this extra covering stop you from getting out and enjoying life. If this makes you feel guilty, then spend a short time thinking about the deceased before you then go and do something new and creative. Doing new things is not denying the importance of the deceased. See it rather as a way of honouring the deceased, in that you are making good come out of a sad situation. Take the deceased with you into the new situation without the past strangling the future.

Dream dreams and write down ideas of things you have always wanted to do and places you have wanted to visit. Start with the simplest and take a friend with you. At first take something tiny with you that will be a bridge with the deceased, e.g. a tie, scarf or a piece of jewellery.

71 *Learn something new*

There is a great reward in learning something new. Anything that you enjoy, that makes you think and gets you excited can only be good for you. It doesn't have to be expensive, it might simply be watching a TV programme on cooking or gardening and then copying it. Bereaved people can become very self-conscious. We worry that we will look foolish or undignified, or we will break down half-way through a new activity and will have to leave. These are natural fears, but you won't be the only one thinking this at a dance or painting class. The teacher will probably be feeling just as nervous. (As a teacher I know that from my own experience.) Although you are highly conscious of your loss, you need to remember that other people can't see or perceive what you are feeling. Equally, you are unaware of the anxiety within other people. Persevere at a new venture for a few weeks, as it can take a while before you can really tell whether it is for you or not.

Find a friend to try out a new experience. Try a one-day taster event. This will feel more manageable than signing up for a year's course. When you start something new, have a quiet word with the leader/teacher so that they can be sensitive to your needs.

72 *Seek out the young*

There is clear evidence that those who remain trapped in their house and don't get back into some kind of routine in the outer world, find it harder to get on with life. I guess that's understandable, but it does mean we have some control of our future. One of the best therapies to look outward is to relate to people younger than yourself. Children are especially good as a catalyst in drawing people out of themselves. They are an example of living for the day, free of worries and fears. By associating with them, we find that we are taken out of ourselves and are able to live more for the day. We can also feel less conscious of ourselves amongst children. This is an important feeling to capture, otherwise we become trapped within ourselves and find it hard to break out.

Is there something you could do to help a local school or playgroup? It might be baking or doing small jobs for the organisation which gets you into an environment that is safe and refreshing.

73 *Body language*

The thought of getting back into the busyness of the world can seem very daunting. It can seem just too big a hurdle to open the door and venture out. The only answer is to break down the barrier bit by bit. When we lose our confidence, it often shows in our body language. We can appear hesitant and withdrawn in company. This is natural as we are anxious we might be asked a question that will upset us. Perhaps we have already had a bad experience. So first make sure that you don't feel trapped. Know where the exits are. But secondly, think through how you are going to react when you meet people. People can only interpret your intentions by what they see or hear you do. Rehearse in your mind that you will move forward to greet people and lean forward so that you look interested. Make eye contact and speak with nods and facial expressions. Don't cross your arms or legs but have an open stance, otherwise you may come across as scared and defensive. This is simply a mind game you have to win. Tell yourself before going out that you 'can and will cope in this situation'. At first it will all feel false but eventually you will find that you are succeeding with less effort and strain.

When you have a special outing or task to perform, make sure you pamper yourself before and afterwards. Have something special to look forward to which can be a target to get you through the task.

74 Allow little hiccups

Life can seem to go one step forward and always two steps back. The good news is that we all have times when life is a struggle and we keep on failing.

As a result of our upbringing, schooling or just our characteristic make-up, we can have a hidden list within our mind by which we judge ourselves. Thoughts such as:

I must do everything perfectly.

I must be approved of by people all of the time.

Criticism proves it's my fault.

The events that happen to me must be entirely my fault.

My loss is my fault. I deserve this.

I'm only worthwhile if someone loves me.

D. W. Winnicot devised the 'good enough principle'. This says that what we have done, whether at work, home or with other people, may not be fantastic, it may not be perfect, it may not be the best, but it is good enough! Try listening to a new tune within you:

I'm trying to be kind to myself.

I'm getting better, one step at a time.

I'm good at my job.

I'm a 'good enough' parent.

I've got a more realistic expectation of life now.

I recognise that crying is not weak but a way of letting myself say what I feel.

Make a list of these positive statements and put them somewhere you will see them as you get up or go out of the house. Remember we will all have lapses. What counts is getting back home and trying again.

75 *Trust your instinct*

When we are confident and life is going well, we are usually very good at trusting our own instinct. However, after a loss we can feel as if our antenna has been snapped. It becomes hard to listen to our inner voice to give us directions. We have to remember that the old self is still within us. We also have the inner thought of what the deceased might well have said to us in a given situation. Try and trust your old instinct. Let it be your indicator for directions, whether it is left or right. After all, we continue to use this instinct to direct us for what is right or wrong within our own moralistic belief system. Think through some of the major decisions you have made in life and the outcomes. Remember, in all your decisions there was timing. So don't feel rushed into decisions you are not ready to make.

Test your instincts out by making a small decision and seeing how it works out. Remember to write the outcome down as a way of reminding yourself that you can trust yourself.

76 *Hopes and aspirations*

It is understandable that after a loss we can lose all sense of the future and any desire to be hopeful. There is a time to dwell on the past and our painful experience, but there is also a time to be positive and to look towards the future. When the day comes when you feel better in yourself, knowing that from experience it might not last too long, give yourself the chance to think creatively for the future. One door has now closed on your life, and we can't undo what has happened, but it doesn't stop us from attempting to open other doors on life. It could be a new hobby or career, or a desire to travel somewhere you have always wanted to go. It could be a desire to produce some goodness in the world through charity action whether as a job or in a voluntary capacity. Write your ideas down. The pendulum will swing back to difficult days, but when it swings back you will be ready to pick up with your thoughts and have an opportunity to push them a little further.

Have a moment to dream dreams and doodle on a piece of paper some of your hopes and wishes. What's stopping you? Remember, all great ideas have started with a simple thought.

77 *Try something at the edge*

Grief can hang over us for such a long time that when we are ready to shake it off, we find it hard to let go. We can be like a tiger that has been stuck in a cage for years pacing up and down and wanting to be free. When the time comes and the cage is opened, the tiger continues to walk up and down as he always has, unable to appreciate the freedom in front of him. Life is such a struggle that we learn to behave in a regular way. It is like wearing an old, familiar jumper that we don't want to get rid of. We expect life to be difficult. We expect to get exhausted each day. We expect the day to be grey. We fail to make the best of our freedom and we behave as if we were still trapped in our grief.

There is only one way of discovering if you are able to shake off the grey clouds. You have to be willing to go out and try new things. Yes, it's risky, but it is riskier to stay as you are and not change. That's a prognosis for depression. We have to accept that life is difficult, things do go wrong, things are unfair, but it mustn't stop us from trying new things. We will only discover what's around the corner if we are willing to go and see.

Try any of these ideas:

Buy yourself some flowers and take in the smell.
Get a book out of the library on a subject you know nothing about.
Try a new hobby or sport.
Join a walking club.
Sign up for a course at the local technical college.
Join a dance class.

I'm sure you can think of lots of reasons why you can't do any of these things but remember, it's the trying that counts.

78 *We all need companions*

If we are going to climb out of the pit we find ourselves in, we will need a friend to journey with us. This is not straightforward. It is easy to discover good friends just don't cope with your grief and so distance themselves from you. Others find themselves fatigued from caring for a bereaved person, as the grief process takes longer than many expect. Sometimes, knowing our need for human compassion, we can share with too many people, hoping that at least one of them will understand.

To find a special friend is a gift. But it is not always easy to receive help and it involves a lot of trust. I have been surprised to find that a lot of bereaved people end up finding someone from a different age group who becomes their main supporter. People surprise you for good or ill. In the end you will need someone who is willing to listen sympathetically to you. Many find support groups helpful where people have had similar experiences. (Contact addresses can be found at No. 101.) Remember, the more you express your thankfulness, the easier it is for the carer.

Who can I trust?

Is there someone I could learn to trust?

Don't get side-tracked by focusing on a person who lets you down. It doesn't mean that there isn't someone out there who could help you.

Positive outcomes

79 *Understanding grief*

When something major happens in our lives that turns everything upside down, it is a natural reaction to want to make sense of it all. There are many books published either about grief theories or of people's own accounts of their grief journey. I will refrain from outlining the theories in detail but will give you three simple pictures.

Some see grief rather like a journey on a train. You get on the grief train and a process happens to you that you seem to have little control over. The train passes through stations called shock, anger, fear, searching and despair. But sooner or later the train arrives at its destination called acceptance, and you get off ready to begin a new life. Others see it rather like a car journey where you are driving. You can control the pace, speed and, to some extent, the direction. Others see it more like a long walk, where for some the journey never ends. Whichever picture relates to you, they are all about a process of change and adjustment. The more you can understand this change, the easier it is to adjust. It can be very beneficial to read accounts of other people's losses. It will help you to see how normal your reaction might be. Although your story is unique, you are not alone in your experience.

How can you use your knowledge and experience to help other people?

80 *Giving thanks and counting your blessings*

Life is full of setbacks and false starts. It is something we have to get used to. We experience grief just as our parents and grandparents before us. Yet there seems to be more depression in our society than ever before. Previous generations were certainly more acquainted with death. There was usually someone within the local street to lay out the deceased. The deceased was kept in the home for all to see. There was also more respect as people paused and removed their hats when the funeral hearse passed. People would alter their clothes, which allowed the community to recognise who was bereaved. All of this enabled people to feel less isolated. But perhaps the biggest difference was that people were more contented with what they had. They certainly had less choice in life but they were able to count their blessings. Many bereaved people I have interviewed have told me that despite their loss, they have learned to appreciate what they have, whether it is health, family or friends or pets.

Can you make a list you want to still be thankful for? See how long you can make it.
Put the list in a prominent place to remind yourself daily. It does not replace the loss in your life but it can be compensation.

81 *No regrets*

The fact is that we all have regrets in life. After all, we have only done this journey once; it is therefore inevitable that along the way there are things we get wrong. Whether it is things we have said in haste or done, we can't put back the clock. But we can do something. First, we can recognise that we are no different from any other human being. We make mistakes, we foul up and we get hurt along with others. Let's not pretend we are any different from anyone else. But, secondly we can do something about how we feel and think. If we have true guilt, it can be acknowledged and forgiven. Whatever your religious background, perhaps a priest could help you. The only way to heal the pain that will not heal itself is to forgive. In the end we have to be willing to forgive ourselves. False guilt needs to be shown up for what it is. Thirdly, although we may feel at rock-bottom, we have some experience behind us to help us climb upwards. We are a little wiser and know there will be good days and hellish days and that we shouldn't make big decisions on bad days. Eventually we must choose to look forward with all that we have learned, or be trapped in looking back.

If you feel you are full of regrets, make a list of them and then make another list of the good things you don't regret. Hopefully, the second should well outnumber the first. Then actively choose to focus upon the positive things you have achieved.

82 *Learning to forgive*

Forgiveness is not an art, but something we have to learn to perform for the good of our health. We have a saying: 'forgive and forget'. Forgetting is a tall order but the two 'f' words are tied together. The more you learn to forgive, the less likely you will dwell upon the events of the past. There is a contrast between those who learn to forgive and those who don't. Lack of forgiveness leads to bitterness and anger. This can often be seen on a person's face. It is difficult to forgive a dead person, or the one who caused the death of a loved one, or an organisation that got things wrong. But by holding on, in the end we are hurting only ourselves. For some people this is what they want. They are punishing themselves. An inability to forgive oneself is often linked to depression. If we can begin to recognise we need to tackle the problem, then it is a start. To start the forgiveness journey we don't have to forgive perfectly. We can still be unsure of what we think and we can still be angry. Secondly, let us recognise there is absolutely nothing we can do that is so bad that it can't be forgiven. Thirdly, the journey will require you to see things from the other person's perspective, however painful that might be. Lastly, forgiveness is a habit; try practising it in small ways.

Is there something I need to forgive myself for?
Do I need to forgive the deceased?
Can I allow others (God, society) to be the judge?
Can I turn all of this energy to good?

83 *Finding a new identity*

As the months go by, there is a point when your life gets back to some kind of routine. We might not want to call it a normal routine, as life can't be the same as before. However, life goes on and we have to find a way of carrying our loved ones with us into the future. For some this means daily reminders, photographs, thoughts about the deceased or even conversations with the deceased. For others, it may simply be at key times remembering and perhaps visiting the grave. There will always be a part of us which will carry our loved ones with us. They do not diminish in our lives; rather we are enlarged to carry them as we embrace the world around us.

However, we also need to learn not to carry baggage we don't require. Just as we take too much on holiday, our excess can weigh us down. It is all too easy to carry grudges and bitterness into the future, which hinder us rather than help us. Our new identity will require us to only hold on to what is necessary for the good of our health and future.

Is it time to have a sort-out of the cupboards and belongings? The things you held on to last year might be less necessary today.

84 *Learning to love yourself*

There are many reasons why we might have a low self-image: a difficult childhood, position in the family, abuse and mistreatment, or just the absence of praise. On top of this, when we are bereaved our self-image and confidence are shaken. We all need acceptance, affection, attention, respect, encouragement and security. We can give some of this to ourselves but we need others to contribute. Unfortunately, when we are bereaved we often push others away, which increases our isolation and in turn lowers our self-image. We may also have lost the very person who believed in us the most. We all need people to care for us, pray for us, and walk with us through life. Although the deceased cannot be replaced, we still need to find a way of being valued. But it begins with yourself. Start physically with eating healthy food and getting plenty of fresh air and exercise. Then make sure you spend time with positive people who give to you rather than drain your energy. Lastly be creative, whether it is writing, painting, gardening or tidying the house. It is as we are creative, especially with others around us, that we discover we are valued.

In the Bible, read Psalm 139 to gain one perspective of yourself.

Take a day off and pamper yourself. Better still, take a friend or a potential friend with you.

85 *Optimist, pessimist or realist?*

We are not all confident about who we are in life. Some of us seem to be born pure optimists while others, for whatever reason, find life hard going. We can't change our genes or our upbringing but we are still in control of the future. Knowing who we are, working within our capacity and yet being willing to stretch ourselves with new challenges, all makes up our true identity. There are times when we behave more like chameleons, presenting a different image depending on who we are with. It is OK to have some friends who you depend on, who will listen and support you, whilst relating to others in a different way. Just don't take the listening friends for granted. They themselves might find energy by caring for others, but in the end all relationships, if they are to last, need a two-way process. There is a time to take stock and to be realistic with your life. Focus on what you are good at and work at improving this. This will help you to feel connected with what really matters to you. Focus upon the things others like about you, on your strengths, the things you get pleasure from. Share your ideas with friends and acquaintances, so that they might support and encourage you.

Set yourself realistic goals that you would like to achieve today, this week, this month and this year. Ask yourself how you can achieve these goals by breaking them down into smaller tasks. Treat yourself with something small each time you reach a target or complete a task. Just drawing a smiley face can lift one's spirit.

86 *Keep looking for new paths*

The world is full of people who will tell you to pull yourself together, accept yourself, forgive and move on, or that the deceased is in a far better place. This book might have had a similar effect. It's OK to be mad with people who just don't understand. Avoid those who pull you down for whatever reason, or have a simple reply that shows you don't agree and that's OK with you. But don't stop trusting people or seeking answers to your questions. One answer does not fit all. Accept that you are on a journey which has many hills and valleys. There are also times when an answer satisfies you temporarily, but it doesn't stop you from searching for a better answer. Life is one long search and there will be some questions that we never find a good enough answer for. But we don't know this without the search. We do know that the journey changes us, usually for the better, and along the way we can become more content in living without the answers. The journey itself becomes more important than the destination.

Practise what to say when someone says something annoying to you, for instance:

'Well, that's interesting, but I don't agree.'
'That's life.'
'Hmm. I really must go now, thanks for the chat.'

Also, have a choice of answers ready when people ask questions connected with the deceased. You will be happy to open up to some people, but sometimes a short answer is more important for your own survival, e.g. with the death of a child you might not want to say you had two children but now have one. It's still true to say you have two children or one child. Make your answer simple, depending on whether you want to explain or not.

87 *Be less materialistic*

Having interviewed several hundred bereaved parents, one of the commonest responses I have found is that the parents tell me they have become less materialistic in their life. A change of priorities has occurred. Promotions, new cars or bigger houses all seem less important when you have lost a child. There is a change of perspective of life. This is true of any major loss in life. We reassess what is important to us, how we spend our time, money and energy. This can be disconcerting to some of our family and friends who tend to want us to stay as we are. But this is an opportunity for you to take a fresh view on life and to make changes that are right for you. If they are not what other people want, then that is their problem not yours. Go with your convictions. Remember, nothing will justify the loss you have experienced, but this does not stop positive things from coming out of the loss. Don't waste the time you have left. Life, as you have discovered, is short and unpredictable, so make the most of your time and see it as a precious commodity.

Make a list of things you would like to do and places you would like to visit. Is there someone who has similar interests you could share this with?

88 *Suffer fools less gladly*

Another area of life that often changes for the bereaved is that they suffer fools less gladly. This is because of a change of perspective of life. Life is no longer as secure as before. Time is more precious and not to be wasted, especially doing things that are now not as important as before. This applies equally to people. So often we put up with long-winded committees that go nowhere and people who talk endlessly about themselves. It becomes hard to be tolerant and patient after a loss. In some ways this is a positive thing. Life, which once stretched out before us, has now been cut short. There is no time to waste, and this message is conveyed to those around us. However, perhaps our eyes have been opened to other people's needs. Have we now gained an understanding when others are struggling with life? Can we identify with them and support them in a new way? Now that we have gained a broader insight into the world, we can bring comfort to others.

Have you noticed how your attitude to people has changed? Can this new awareness be used in some capacity for the good of others?

89 *Special places*

There are times in life when we need to put up a sign that says, 'gone for lunch'. Just as we all need to eat, we equally need times for space for ourselves to think and ponder. It might simply be going to the local park, garden, library or church. For some, it is visiting the grave of a loved one or visiting a place that has fond memories for you. Wherever it is, we all need an oasis. Visit it as often as you feel the need. In the early days of loss you may need a safe place at home where you can hide away from all the pressures. Relatives may not appreciate your need and may feel you are being self-centred. But the world and your family will survive. Remember, this is a time when you can be kind to yourself. Eventually you can find new special places, perhaps on holiday, which you can share with others. You may find that you now require more breaks away from the routine to top up your battery and to gain equilibrium. Allow yourself this privilege. A car can't run without fuel and you are no different. And when you find others in need, why not share your places of discovery and be a blessing to others?

Ask your local minister of religion if they can suggest places of oasis. If you are retreating at home to escape the pressure around, pop a note on your door explaining you need some space.

90 *Make time for the best*

When the jigsaw of life has been thrown up in the air, it can be hard to see the whole picture. Things get muddled up in our mind. So much so, that we can fail to recognise when we have a good day. It is so easy to allow days to blur together with no distinction between them. We have to make a habit of recognising the better days among the mundane ones. When they occur, and only you can recognise them, you need to acknowledge them. Perhaps this will involve telephoning a friend or relative, writing it down in a diary or marking the calendar, or simply treating yourself to something nice like chocolate or a favourite drink. By marking the occasion, we allow ourselves to recognise that things are not static but gradually improving.

This doesn't mean that the next day will be equally good or that we can reproduce such experiences at will. But it does remind us that we are on a journey upwards and onwards. Life is still unpredictable and at times unfair, but along the way there are moments that just about make it all worthwhile.

Have you forgotten to recognise good moments? Begin to mark your calendar with a star when something positive happens. Write and tell a friend that you had a good day. It will encourage you as well as your friend. Remember, the more you talk about positive events, the more they seem to occur.

91 *This is me*

Whatever you looked like before you experienced the death of someone close to you, you will look, feel and think differently as the months go by. This is all part of the rich tapestry of life. There are times when our lives look more like the back of the tapestry rather than the front. We look and all we can see is a lot of loose threads with no pattern at all. But this is now a part of your life story. Much of the tapestry is now complete and can't be changed. We need to accept this as the 'warp and weft' of our life. It all contributes to making us a unique human being with our own personal experience. We can't live many lives, only one. What we can do is to accept what has come to us and choose to make the most of the tapestry of life yet to be completed. Those around us have to take us as we are. People will want us to be many things, for good and ill reasons, but we have to find a peace in just being ourselves, warts and all. If others can't accept us as we are, then at least we can attempt to accept ourselves and find something within us to love.

Is it time to place less importance on what others want of you and to focus upon what you really want to do with your life?
Give yourself credit that you have travelled this far and survived.

Finally

92 *Am I really ill?*

First, let us recognise that grieving is not an illness, even though it has the same feeling. Grief is a natural process that happens universally to anyone who experiences the loss of someone special. It varies across the world due to cultural mourning rituals that we pick up from our environment. However, the fact that it is not classed as an illness doesn't lessen the impact upon us. It is very common for the bereaved to visit the doctor more often. The emotional impact of loss naturally affects us physically. So don't be surprised if you find that your sleeping and eating patterns are disturbed and you find yourself with aches and pains. You may well feel at times that your emotions get the better of you and you might think you are going mad! We can do the strangest of things in grief. I've heard from people who have suddenly broken every pot plant in the house or have suddenly decided to strip all the walls bare of wallpaper. Meeting other people with similar losses can help you to realise that your experience is not unusual and you are not alone.

Find a friendly doctor who has an open-door approach and don't be afraid to visit the surgery.
Remember, bereaved people are just normal; they get ill like anybody else.
Find a bereavement support group who can help you through the difficult times (No. 101).

93 *Professional help*

However supportive your family and the local community might be, there are times when we all need some additional help. It can be encouraging to have someone outside your support group who can look at the situation with fresh eyes. Finding the right help can be complex, as there is a range of different types of counsellors practising, but there are a few simple rules. First, see if a friend can recommend someone. Personal recommendation is better than finding a counsellor out of a phone book. Secondly, if the help is being provided by the NHS and is not going to be financially too much, then it is worth pursuing. Thirdly, if what is on offer is purely medication, be aware you may need additional help to work through issues. Fourthly, is the counsellor friendly and do they understand where you are coming from? If not, then ditch them and find another. Finally, don't get hooked on counselling support. It works best in small doses. If you are paying, be aware that the counsellor might want you to stick around longer than necessary.

Look at the back of the book at the list of agencies that will help you find a counsellor.
Before beginning with counselling, find out what qualifications the person has, whether they are affiliated with a counselling agency and whether they have insurance.

94 *Who to trust*

Trusting people is a tricky business at the best of times, let alone when you feel under the weather. However, we do have a lot of experience at our fingertips. Who has been there for you previously? Is there anyone offering help with no strings attached? Accept the fact that someone who was previously helpful to you may just find the loss issue too much for them to cope with. They are not your problem; move on until you find someone who can cope with you. Others will help a lot at first but gradually fall away. This is just how it is, so be glad that they were there for you for a period at least.

With counsellors, remember it takes great courage to be willing to see someone in the first place and it can take a while for you to trust them enough to open up with your story. All therapy is painful; don't let that be a reason for giving up on it. Find someone who is willing to work with the issues you want to deal with rather than their own agenda. If they want to explore other areas of your life, ask for an explanation. If you are not convinced, then say so, or if that's too difficult, give up the sessions. Remember, it is about you being in control of the situation, not family, friends or counsellors.

Very few people can journey with us the whole of the way. Look back and recognise those who have been helpful to you at different points in time.
Why not drop them a note and say thank you?
Is it time for you to offer support to another person? We don't have to be all sorted out to help others. The best helpers are people who also know that they too need help.

95 *Complex losses – suicide*

When someone takes their own life, they leave behind extra baggage for the bereaved to deal with. There are always the questions 'Why?' and 'Could I have done something about it?' But with suicide these questions are heightened. One might wonder about how well they knew the person in light of their actions. There is also the awkwardness of what to tell people, coupled with the fear that we ourselves or another member of the family might also follow suit with suicidal thoughts, and how to handle the anger we might feel towards the deceased. There are no easy answers to these questions. Part of the solution is in coming to terms with the fact that we will never have all the answers we are searching for. In such circumstances, there is often the need to talk to someone outside the family. Help is often necessary to assist an individual or family to get beyond the big question of 'why' so that other grief issues might be discussed. We need to remind ourselves that although we can feel angry and upset with the deceased, this does not remove our love and appreciation of them. With so many difficult questions and thoughts, it can be a relief to share them with someone and to have the feedback that we are just normal. We are probably experiencing similar reactions to many bereaved individuals who have seen someone special to them take their own life.

Every individual exercises choice within their own life. Just as this person has chosen to end their life, you have the choice to learn from it and to make the most of yours.

Try and write a letter to the deceased about your feelings and questions. Just writing them down can help to release them from the mind.

Decide what you will tell people when they ask. If in doubt, say something like, 'He/she died in tragic circumstances.' You don't have to talk further if you don't want to.

96 *Complex losses – murder*

When a murder occurs, we not only have to deal with our sudden loss but many other issues also engulf us. There is the involvement of the police who quite rightly have to consider whether we had anything to do with the person's death. Along with this, there is always a high press and media interest. We also have to deal with the attention given to finding the killer. This process can be long and drawn out. Even if the killer is caught, there is then a long wait until the trial, with the chance that the person might be acquitted and the search begin again. Even if the killer is sent to prison, there is the concern about how long their sentence will be and whether they might be released early. It can seem that there are just so many things going on that we hardly get round to grieving for ourselves. There is a point when we need to leave the justice side of it all to the police and give our rightful attention to the deceased and ourselves. We need time to work through our thoughts about the deceased, their past and our time with them. We also need to have time to focus especially upon our own needs; after all we are victims too in the situation.

Find a friend who can take you out of the context of it all and help you to get a better perspective on life. Make a decision of just how long you are willing to focus upon the issues of the death and set a time when you will actively choose to move on with your life. It will always be with you, but you can choose how much it will dominate.

97 *Complex losses – child loss*

The loss of a child turns the life of a parent upside down. Whether it is a baby or a 25-year-old son or daughter, the impact is enormous. It affects siblings, grandparents and the wider community. The reality is that parents go on grieving for the child till the day they themselves die. It is so easy for this loss to consume you to such an extent that you neglect your other children, partner and yourself. There is often so great a longing to be with the deceased that suicidal thoughts are not uncommon. For most bereaved parents, not a day goes by when they don't think about their child. The answer has to be in finding a way of carrying the deceased child with you into the future whilst not diminishing your own life. We have to be able to remember the deceased whilst not idealising them. This can make it impossible for siblings to live up to the imagined reputation of the deceased who never seemed to do any wrong. The truth is, we can't say what our child would have become or what heartache they might have caused us. What we can do is to be thankful for knowing them, find ways of remembering them and attempt to bring something good out of it. It will never compensate for our loss, but will bring a richness in spite of it.

Find people who you can talk to about your child, using his or her name. Allow yourself special times to focus upon your loss, thus releasing you to get on with other things in the gaps.

98 Look how far you have travelled

It is good to look back and see how far you have travelled in your grief. Things will have changed; some for the better and perhaps some for the worse. Nevertheless, you are not where you started when you opened this book. Inevitably, time will have taken you further away from some of your memories of the deceased. But hopefully there are other compensations. Perhaps your life is more honest, more based in reality. If nothing else, you have survived a period of time that you couldn't see a way through. Perhaps you can't remember the worst parts of the journey now. It's as if things were so bad that our defences have protected us by removing the pain.

The journey of grief has many tunnels. There are moments when we think we have come through it, into the light, only to find that there is another tunnel up ahead. But gradually there are fewer tunnels, and whether we feel like it or not, the road takes us forward. We must go on and, although the road up ahead is unclear, having come this far, surely we can face what lies around the corner?

If need be, go back to the beginning and read through the book again. Keep doing it until it is not necessary.

What were the most helpful tips in this book? Mark them down so that they might encourage you in the future.

If you have kept a diary, is now the time to read through it?

Pop a note to someone to say thank you for journeying with you.

99 *Lessons learned*

I hope you have now realised that the deceased has not been left far behind on your journey. He or she has journeyed with you, shaping and influencing you. They are always a part of you and will never be far from your thoughts. But your life has also grown from this experience. You have learned new skills of survival; you have discovered who your true friends are, and you are learning not to hang on to bitterness and regrets. You have recognised that life brings fluctuations in your moods, and that it is normal to go one step forward and two steps back. Finally, you have realised that life is tough, but you just about have a handle on it. Well done, congratulate yourself. Remember, however you view the past, the future has not yet been written. It's up to you to make something good of the future. Have a go!

Go on practising all the skills you have learned on this journey. Perhaps you could pass them on to someone else along the way?
If you would like to share what has helped you the most, what have been the difficult times for you, or any other words of wisdom, do e-mail me at
support@counsellingcare.org
I will try to acknowledge any correspondence.
Any contributions will go towards further research into how we can support those in grief.

100 ~ *Find a retreat*

The Retreat Association (They have a journal which will direct you to the nearest retreat house and give you an idea of the range of different types of retreats available.)
Tel. 0845 456 1429
www.retreats.org.uk

101 ⁓ *Find support*

The Samaritans
Tel. 08457 90 90 90
www.samaritans.org.uk

Cruse Bereavement Care
Tel. 020 8939 9530
www.crusebereavementcare.org.uk

The Compassionate Friends
Tel. 0845 123 2304
www.tcf.org.uk
To look at their list of library books contact:
tcf.postallibrary@btinternet.com

Mental Health Matters
www.mentalhealth.org.uk

Association of Christian Counsellors
Tel. 0845 124 9569
www.acc-uk.org

British Association of Counsellors and Psychotherapists
Tel. 0870 443 5252
www.bacp.co.uk

Edward's Trust (a child bereavement support in the West Midlands)
Tel. 0121 456 4838
www.edwardstrust.org.uk

Winston's Wish (child bereavement support)
Tel. 0845 20 30 40 5
www.winstonswish.org.uk

If you require further advice, contact me at
support@counsellingcare.org

Also by Bill Merrington:

Suffering Love – how parents cope with the death of children

Coping with the Sudden Death of a Parent
(previously known as The Hideaway)

Coping with the Death of a Parent through Illness
(previously known as Alice's Dad)

First Response to Grief and Loss –
a manual and DVD for professional workers
engaging with children and young people (2006)

Coping When Your Parents Separate –
the adventures of Tabatha and Skimble (2007)